P9-CCT-894

PRESIDENTS OF THE U.S.A.

GERALD R. FORD
OUR THIRTY-EIGHTH PRESIDENT

by Sandra Francis

THE CHILD'S WORLD ®

Published in the United States of America

The Child's World®
1980 Lookout Drive • Mankato, MN 56003-1705
800-599-READ • www.childsworld.com

Acknowledgments
The Child's World®: Mary Berendes, Publishing Director

The Creative Spark: Mary McGavic, Project Director; Shari Joffe, Editorial
Director; Deborah Goodsite, Photo Research; Nancy Ratkiewich, Page Production

The Design Lab: Kathleen Petelinsek, Design

Content Adviser: Gleaves Whitney, Director, Hauenstein Center for Presidential
Studies, Grand Valley State University, Allendale, Michigan

Photos
Cover and page 3: Courtesy Gerald R. Ford Library

Interior: The Art Archive: 10 (National Archives, Washington DC); Associated
Press Images: 21 (Henry Griffin), 27 (file photo); Corbis: 12 (Victor Jorgensen),
18 and 38, 25 (Corbis), 29, 30 and 39 (Bettmann); Gerald R. Ford Library:
4, 5, 6, 7, 9, 13, 14, 17, 19, 20, 24, 32 (David Hume Kennerly, White House
Photograph); Getty Images: 8, 36 (Getty), 11, 33 (Time & Life Pictures), 34
(Stephen Jaffe/AFP); The Image Works: 28 and 38 (Mark Godfrey); iStockphoto:
44 (Tim Fan); Landov: 35 (Reuters/David Hume Kennerly/White House);
SuperStock: 22 (National Portrait Gallery, London); U.S. Air Force photo: 45.

Library of Congress Cataloging-in-Publication Data
Francis, Sandra.
  Gerald R. Ford / by Sandra Francis.
     p. cm.— (Presidents of the U.S.A.)
  Includes bibliographical references and index.
  ISBN 978-1-60253-066-9 (library bound : alk. paper)
1. Ford, Gerald R., 1913–2006—Juvenile literature. 2. Presidents—United
States—Biography—Juvenile literature. I. Title.

E866.F69 2008
973.925092—dc22
   [B]
                                                    2007049070

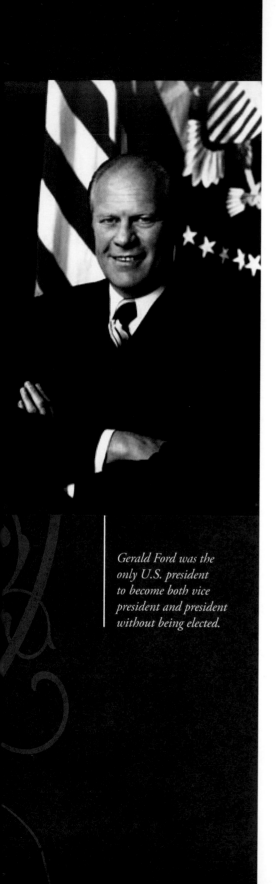

Gerald Ford was the only U.S. president to become both vice president and president without being elected.

TABLE OF CONTENTS

CHAPTER ONE

HAPPY CHILDHOOD

Gerald R. Ford's childhood was a happy one, but it did have an unusual beginning. He was born in Omaha, Nebraska, on July 14, 1913. His parents were Leslie Lynch King and Dorothy Gardner King. They named their new son Leslie Lynch King Jr.

Gerald R. Ford was born on July 14, 1913. Here he is shown with his dog.

From the start of the marriage, Mr. King had been an unkind husband. Two weeks after little Leslie's birth, Dorothy and her son left home. They went to live with her parents in Grand Rapids, Michigan. Soon Dorothy and Leslie King were divorced, and Dorothy had full care of her beautiful, blond-haired baby boy.

Dorothy and "Junie," as she called her son, enjoyed a happy new beginning. One day at a church social, Dorothy met a wonderful man named Gerald R. Ford. He was nice to her and to Junie. He was successful and owned his own paint business. After a year of dating, Gerald and Dorothy married on February 1, 1916.

Gerald loved Junie as if he were his own child. As Junie grew up, his family began to call him Jerry and then Gerald R. Ford Jr. Over the years, the Fords had three more sons: Thomas, Richard, and James. The Fords were a close, happy family. In fact, until Jerry was a teenager, he did not know that Gerald R. Ford Sr. was not his real father. Many years later, in 1935, Jerry officially changed his name to Gerald R. Ford Jr.

Jerry's years at South High School in Grand Rapids were busy ones. He was not only an excellent student, but a popular athlete as well. Good grades earned him membership in the school's honor society. Although

Ford said he was very lucky to have a strong, happy family during his childhood. Here, young Jerry holds the reins of a pioneer wagon during a neighborhood parade.

Jerry Ford (far left) was very active during his high-school years. One thing he enjoyed was scouting. At age 14, he achieved the rank of Eagle Scout. In the summer of 1929, he and his troop served as guides at a scout camp. There he discovered that he liked meeting people and being a leader.

Jerry was voted the most popular senior at his high school.

Even though Jerry Ford was born left-handed, his teachers made him write with his right hand (it was common at the time for teachers to do this). Ford developed a stutter in his speech. Finally, his teachers let him write with his left hand, and the stuttering stopped.

Jerry dreamed of becoming a famous baseball player, he was even better at football. His skill on the playing field earned him spots on the All-City and All-State football teams. After practice and on weekends, Jerry earned spending money working at the family business. He also worked at a local restaurant.

When Jerry was ready to enter college, the family did not have enough money to pay for it. The Great Depression had brought hard times to the country and to the Ford family. The Depression was a period in U.S. history when there was little business activity. Many people could not find work. In these rough times, Jerry's good grades and athletic ability paid off. The principal of his high school arranged for Jerry to receive a scholarship, an award that would help pay for school. Jerry later said that this "was the luckiest break I ever had." In 1931, he enrolled at the University of Michigan at Ann Arbor.

Over the next four years, Jerry earned good grades. He was also a football star and played on the school's national championship teams in 1932 and 1933. He was voted the most valuable player in 1934. Jerry still needed to earn extra money, however. While at the university, he took several jobs to help pay his expenses. All this hard work paid off. It led the way to many rewards, both in college and in his future. In June of 1935, Jerry graduated from the University of Michigan.

One of Jerry's next goals was to study law at Yale University, one of the nation's best schools. Money for education was still difficult to come by, and he knew he would have to continue working. He found a job coaching football and boxing at Yale and hoped this would help him earn enough money to pay for school. But it wasn't easy. At first, Yale Law School did not accept him. Many people wanted to attend Yale. The school accepted only one out of every four students

Jerry Ford was the first U.S. president to have been an Eagle Scout.

Ford was once a park ranger at Yellowstone National Park in Wyoming.

Jerry (second from left) was very close to his stepfather. This photograph shows him as a teenager with his stepfather and half brothers on the front steps of their home.

Jerry is shown here in 1934, when he was voted the most valuable player of the University of Michigan's football team. After graduating, he received offers to play for two professional teams: the Detroit Lions and the Green Bay Packers. Jerry turned down the offers. His dream was to become a lawyer.

Jerry's high-school coach gave him this advice: "You play to win. You give it everything you've got, but you always play within the rules." Jerry remembered and applied this advice throughout his life.

who applied, usually those with the highest grades. Jerry's grades were good, but they weren't the very best. In addition, Jerry was working full-time as a coach. The Yale professors thought he would be too busy with his job to work hard at his studies.

Jerry didn't give up. In the summer of 1937, he took more courses at the University of Michigan. The following spring, he presented Yale with his good grades. Jerry had earned his way into one of the best schools in the country! He completed his law degree in 1941. Even though he still worked full-time as a coach, he graduated in the top 25 percent of his class.

Jerry returned to Michigan to set up a law practice in Grand Rapids. His partner was a college friend, Philip A. Buchen. As always, Jerry kept very busy. He taught a course in business law at the University of Grand Rapids and coached the school's football team. He also became active in the **Republican Party,** one of the nation's two most powerful **political parties.**

But about six months later, on December 7, 1941, Gerald Ford's career was interrupted. While driving home from his office, he heard very bad news. Japanese warplanes had attacked the U.S. naval base in Pearl Harbor, Hawaii. This violent act forced the United States to enter World War II, and the nation would need its young men to go to battle.

As a high-school senior, Jerry was selected for a school trip to Washington, D.C. There he got his first glimpse of the government at work.

The Japanese attack on Pearl Harbor killed more than 2,400 Americans, sank or damaged 18 U.S. ships, and destroyed or damaged more than 200 U.S. airplanes.

Jerry (right) and his fellow football coaches are shown preparing for practice at Yale University in 1935. Jerry accepted the coaching job hoping that he would one day attend Yale Law School. His dream came true in 1938.

PEARL HARBOR

Before World War II, the United States rarely became involved with the affairs of other countries. Americans preferred to stay out of problems around the world, a policy known as **isolationism**. But then Germany's **Nazi Party**, led by Adolf Hitler, came to power in the early 1930s. Soon it threatened to take over all of Europe.

At the same time, Japan was aggressively attacking other Asian nations. On December 7, 1941, the Japanese bombed Pearl Harbor (above), the U.S. naval base in Hawaii. This act killed 2,403 Americans and wounded more than 1,000. The next day, the United States declared war. It could no longer remain isolated from other countries. To protect its people and its shores, the U.S. went to war.

World War II changed Gerald Ford's view of the world, as well as the views of other Americans. "Before the war I was a typical Midwest isolationist," he once said. "I returned understanding we could never be isolated again. We were and are one world. It was clear to me, it was inevitable to me, that this country was obligated to lead in this new world. We had won the war. It was up to us to keep the peace."

CHAPTER TWO

ABOARD THE USS *MONTEREY*

The bombing of Pearl Harbor changed the world forever. Less than a week after the attack, Gerald R. Ford applied to become part of the active naval reserve. His desire was to be part of the intelligence branch of the navy. To do so, he had to pass a background check. This took months to complete and the navy could not promise that he would be accepted.

Finally, in April of 1942, Ford entered basic training. He accepted a position as an **ensign** and began training at the U.S. Naval Academy. After he completed his training period, Ford was quickly **promoted** from ensign to lieutenant. His first assignment was as the athletic training **officer** at the preflight school in North Carolina. His job was to teach the navy's future pilots physical fitness, seamanship, and gunnery. Although this assignment was not what Ford wanted,

Gerald Ford joined the U.S. Navy in 1942.

In 1943, Ford began service on the USS Monterey *in the South Pacific. The ship's crew took part in many of the major battles in the Pacific during World War II. This photo shows an airplane taking off from the* Monterey.

he did his best. His commanding officer said Ford was "an outstanding officer, one of the finest in the station, and an excellent shipmate."

Finally, in 1943, the navy assigned Ford to sea duty on the USS *Monterey.* The *Monterey* was an **aircraft carrier** that had been rebuilt for combat. It could carry more than 1,500 sailors and 45 bomber and fighter aircraft.

In October, the *Monterey* was ready to go into battle. It joined Admiral Halsey's Third Fleet in the South Pacific. The crew of the *Monterey* first saw action on November 19, 1943, when its planes fired on a Japanese base in the Gilbert Islands. The battle lasted for three weeks. Ford's job was to stand at the back of the ship and tell soldiers when and where to fire their guns. He later remembered that his battle experiences were terrifying. "The Japanese planes came after us with a vengeance," he said.

Ford made friends with Captain Lester Hundt, a great football fan. This friendship soon led to Ford's new position as the assistant **navigator,** although he had no training in navigation. But with the teaching of Commander Pappy Atwood, Ford learned the job quickly. He liked his new position. He was in the middle of the action, where navy leaders made important decisions.

Beginning in January of 1944, the *Monterey* and its crew were in many major battles. They attacked enemy ships and shores. Japanese pilots came after all

Ford is shown here (seated second from right) with other gunnery officers aboard the Monterey. *Their job was to tell soldiers when and where to fire their guns.*

Ford helped build a basketball court on *the* **hangar deck** *of the* Monterey. *He knew that exercise would keep the men in good condition and in good spirits. Here he leaps to block a shot.*

the U.S. aircraft carriers and cruisers in the region. One day, a torpedo meant for the *Monterey* narrowly missed it. The *Monterey* fought off its Japanese attackers for 24 hours straight. The mangled U.S. cruisers sailed away from the battle, but the *Monterey* was still going strong. It attacked its enemy one more time, allowing the cruisers to escape. In just a little over a year, the *Monterey* and its crew of brave men earned 10 battle stars (special honors).

Surviving all that the enemy could throw at the *Monterey* was just the beginning. In December of 1944, the crew faced something that became even more dangerous than enemy fire. What became known as the

Great Typhoon was one of the worst storms ever seen in the Pacific Ocean. Commander Atwood issued an immediate order to tie the planes tightly to the deck. The crew of the *Monterey* could see other ships being tossed around like toys, then sinking into the furious ocean. Picking up survivors was almost impossible, and many lives were lost to the storm.

Lieutenant Ford awoke to the smell of smoke. Grabbing his helmet, he tried to reach his battle station. "As I stepped on the flight deck, the ship suddenly rolled about 25 degrees. I lost my footing, fell to the deck flat on my face, and started sliding toward the port [left] side as if I were on a toboggan slide," he later recalled.

Ford slid, feet first, 109 feet (33 m) across the flight deck. As his body rushed toward the sea, he spotted a rim of metal that went around the deck. "I put out my feet and hit it," Ford later remembered. "Instead of going over the side, I twisted my body as my feet hit the rim, and I landed in the narrow catwalk just below the port edge of the flight deck."

The water rushed by him only two feet (about 1 m) away. Ford clung to the rim until he caught his breath. He managed to pull himself back up and ran to his battle station. What he saw was disaster. Airplanes had been torn loose, and fires were spreading from the front to the back of the ship. "The planes bounded around the hangar deck like trapped and terrified birds," he said. "Showers of sparks flew as the planes crashed into each other and against the sides of the ship."

As the Great Typhoon raged, the winds were reported to be about 124 miles (200 km) per hour. Waves reached heights of nearly 100 feet (30 m).

Ford remained in the U.S. Naval Reserves until 1963. This meant that in the event of a war, he could have been called into action.

Working feverishly, the crew pushed torpedoes, bombs, and other explosives overboard. Only one of the ship's engines was working, and it couldn't carry all this weight. There was little water pressure in the hoses, so fighting the fires was difficult. Struggling bravely, the crew battled the raging sea to keep the *Monterey* upright.

A radio message from Admiral Halsey ordered them to abandon ship. Nearby cruisers were waiting to rescue the crew. Commander Atwood refused to abandon the ship. He asked Halsey for more time to save the *Monterey.* For another 40 minutes, Atwood and the brave crew struggled to get the ship upright in the fierce wind. This reduced the ship's motion so the crew could put out the fires without dodging the airplanes. Atwood's plan to save the ship and his men was successful. Seven hours later, the *Monterey* found its way to a safe harbor in the western Caroline Islands. When it was all over, three men had died and 40 more were injured. The navy determined that the ship was unfit for further service. It was taken out of the water for major repairs.

Even after this frightening experience, Ford still wanted to be assigned to sea duty. Instead, he was ordered back to the United States and promoted. Ford's service report stated, "He is steady, reliable, and resourceful. . . . His unfailing good humor, pleasing personality, and natural ability as a leader made him well liked and respected by the officers and men." These qualities had always been typical of Ford, and they would continue to be throughout his life.

Although the Monterey's *crew faced many dangerous battles with the enemy, the worst event of all was the typhoon that struck in December of 1944. Ford almost lost his life in the violent storm. This photograph shows the* Monterey *tipping during that storm.*

Ford was a member of the American Legion, the Veterans of Foreign Wars, and AMVETS. All of these are organizations for people who have served in the U.S. military.

Ford was assigned to the U.S. Navy Training Command in Glenview, Illinois. He was to train new officers for duty at sea and in the air. Ford wished to enter into combat again and applied for a position on a ship called the *Coral Sea*. But Japan surrendered on August 14, 1945. World War II was over, and Ford was **discharged** from the navy the following February.

WEDDING DAY

In August of 1947, friends introduced Ford to Betty Bloomer Warren. She was a former model and dancer who worked as a fashion coordinator at a large department store. Ford liked Betty's energy and honesty. But although he admired her, he had little time for dating. He was determined to have a career in **politics**. Ford later said that when he met Betty, he "had no idea that someone special had just come into my life." Betty felt the same way. She liked Ford but also led a busy life. They saw each other occasionally, but both agreed not to take their friendship too seriously.

That Christmas, Ford traveled to Idaho for a ski vacation, and Betty attended fashion shows in New York City. The separation made them realize how much they missed each other. The following February, Ford proposed. "I'd like to marry you," was how he put it, "but we can't get married until next fall." He had promised to keep his **campaign** for Congress a secret and could not even tell his future wife. Finally, his plans became public, and Betty even helped with the campaign. On October 15th, less than a month before the election, Ford and Betty were married. In this photograph, the happy couple stands outside Grace Episcopal Church in Grand Rapids after the wedding ceremony.

CHAPTER THREE

A STRONG START

Returning to Grand Rapids after four years of military duty, Ford accepted a position with one of the best law firms in town. Julius Amberg, a senior partner at the firm, took Ford under his wing. He taught him how to be the best business lawyer he could be. Ford did not disappoint his employers. He was the first one to arrive at work in the morning and the last one to leave at night.

Ford became known for his honesty and hard work. This linked him to many important people who would help him succeed. Although he considered himself lucky, Ford also had faith in his abilities. He never forgot his father's words, "Hard work brings good luck." Ford was willing to work hard, and his practice of honesty earned him the trust of powerful people.

Ford returned to Michigan in 1946 and took a job at a Grand Rapids law firm. He became very active in the community.

In 1948, Ford decided to enter politics. He entered the race for a seat in the U.S. House of Representatives. Here Ford is shown chatting with voters during a campaign stop at a Michigan farm.

Both Ford and his wife had been models before their marriage.

Ford accidentally wore one brown shoe and one black shoe to his wedding.

In 1948, Ford decided to run for the U.S. House of Representatives, which is part of Congress. To win the office, he had to challenge Bartel J. Jonkman, who had been in the House for 10 years. Like Ford, Jonkman was a Republican. To enter the general election, Ford had to win the **nomination** of the Republican Party.

Ford asked John Stiles, a former classmate and writer, to be his campaign manager. Neither Ford nor Stiles had any experience in politics, the work of the government. But together they created a plan to put

Ford into office. Ford did not tell anyone he planned to be a **candidate** until the last minute. That way, Jonkman and his supporters would not have much time to campaign against him. The plan worked, and the Republicans chose Ford as their candidate. He then went on to win the general election on November 2, 1948, with 61 percent of the vote. Ford took his seat in the House of Representatives the following January.

During Ford's first days in Congress, he met Richard Nixon, a well-known representative from California. Nixon approached Ford with a handshake

Before the election of 1948, Ford made a campaign promise. He said that if he won the election, he would work at a dairy farm for two weeks. He kept his promise: "There I was, every morning . . . helping with the cows, cleaning up the barn, you name it."

Jerry and Betty Ford stand in front of the U.S. Capitol soon after Ford's election to Congress in 1948.

WORDS OF WISDOM

Ford's favorite poem was "If," by Rudyard Kipling (above).
The poem put into words how Ford lived his life.

If

By Rudyard Kipling

If you can keep your head when all about you
Are losing theirs and blaming it on you;
If you can trust yourself when all men doubt you,
But make allowance for their doubting too;
If you can wait and not be tired by waiting,
Or, being lied about, don't deal in lies,
Or, being hated, don't give way to hating,
And yet don't look too good, nor talk too wise;

If you can dream—and not make dreams your master;
If you can think—and not make thoughts your aim;
If you can meet with triumph and disaster
And treat those two imposters just the same;
If you can bear to hear the truth you've spoken
Twisted by knaves to make a trap for fools,
Or watch the things you gave your life to broken,
And stoop and build 'em up with wornout tools;

If you can make one heap of all your winnings
And risk it on one turn of pitch-and-toss,
And lose, and start again at your beginnings
And never breath a word about your loss;
If you can force your heart and nerve and sinew
To serve your turn long after they are gone,
And so hold on when there is nothing in you
Except the Will which says to them: "Hold on";

If you can talk with crowds and keep your virtue,
Or walk with kings—nor lose the common touch;
If neither foes nor loving friends can hurt you;
If all men count with you, but none too much;
If you can fill the unforgiving minute
With sixty seconds' worth of distance run—
Yours is the Earth and everything that's in it,
And—which is more—you'll be a Man my son!

When Ford served in Congress, the Ford family divided their time between a home in Grand Rapids and one in Alexandria, Virginia. The Fords had four children (from left to right): Susan, Jack, Michael, and Steven.

While running for Congress in 1948, Ford even campaigned on his wedding day.

and congratulated him on his big win in the election. Ford was surprised that Nixon—or anyone—had heard of him. Nixon became a longtime friend, as well as an important step in Ford's path to the presidency.

From the start, Ford promised himself that he would not allow other Republicans to pressure him into making decisions. Instead, he wanted to make decisions for himself. His friendly personality and firm beliefs allowed him to disagree with others without making enemies. These qualities made him a successful **politician.** In fact, Ford spent the next

24 years in the House of Representatives. He was so respected in this position that the people of Michigan reelected him 12 times. In every election, he always won more than 60 percent of the vote.

During his years in the House, Ford held many important positions. In 1951, he became a member of the House Appropriations Committee. This committee makes decisions about how the government should raise and spend money. In 1961, he became a member of the Defense Appropriations Subcommittee. This committee determines how the military should spend its money. Many people encouraged Ford to run for the Senate or to try to become the governor of Michigan. He always refused. His goal was to become the Speaker of the House, the leader of the House of Representatives.

During his early years as a congressman, Jerry Ford kept his office in a mobile home. Citizens were welcome to visit the office to meet with Ford and discuss their concerns.

In 1963, President John F. Kennedy was **assassinated.** His vice president, Lyndon Johnson, then became president. Johnson named Ford to the Warren Commission. The commission's job was to investigate the death of President Kennedy. In 1965, Ford and his friend John Stiles wrote a book about the investigation, *Portrait of the Assassin.*

Ford was the first person to become vice president because the elected vice president had resigned.

In 1965, Ford was elected to the position of **minority** leader of the House of Representatives. In this post, he represented the Republicans in the House. The Republicans were the minority because they had fewer members in the House than the Democrats did at the time. Ford held the position for almost nine years. As minority leader, he traveled around the country and gave more than 200 speeches each year. He became well known. Throughout his time in Congress, Ford always had good relations with other politicians, even those with whom he disagreed.

When Richard Nixon ran for president in 1968, Ford supported him. Nixon won that election, and the one in 1972 as well. During President Nixon's second **term,** Vice President Spiro Agnew **resigned** from office after being accused of tax evasion, not paying money he owed to the government. Nixon had to choose a new vice president. Ford, the honest, well-liked congressman from Michigan, seemed to be a good choice. The FBI ran its most thorough investigation in history on Gerald Ford. He passed the test and was approved quickly. Ford was sworn into office as the new vice president on December 6, 1973.

All was not well, however. President Nixon faced another, more serious problem: the Watergate **scandal.** Before the election of 1972, Nixon supporters had broken into the Democratic Party's offices at the Watergate Hotel in Washington, D.C. They went there to steal information to help Nixon beat the Democratic candidate in the election. The

burglars were caught, and members of Nixon's staff went to jail.

All along, Nixon claimed that he had played no part in these illegal activities. But more and more evidence pointed toward Nixon's involvement in covering up the scandal. Congress prepared to **impeach** the president. Before that could happen, Nixon became the first U.S. president to resign from office.

On August 9, 1974, eight months after he became vice president, Gerald Ford became president

Ford supported his friend Richard Nixon in two presidential elections. Here he stands near Nixon (right) as Nixon accepts his party's nomination at the 1968 Republican National Convention.

On August 9, 1974, Ford was sworn in as the 38th president of the United States. Ford said goodbye to Richard Nixon as the former president left the White House. "That was very sad because of our long personal friendship," Ford later recalled.

of the United States. At his **inauguration,** Ford said, "I assume the presidency under extraordinary circumstances. . . . This is an hour of history that troubles our minds and hurts our hearts." He knew his task would be to heal a nation hurt by a president's dishonesty, and it would not be easy.

THE PRESIDENCY

In the summer of 1974, the stunned American people had watched as Nixon resigned from office, giving up the presidency. Americans had lost faith in him and in their government. Against this backdrop, Nixon's vice president, Gerald Ford, took the oath of office on August 9, 1974.

Ford may have been the perfect person to take office at that time. As he entered office, he told Americans that "the long national nightmare" was over. Right away, he wanted to prove that his personal qualities and goals were very different from those of President Nixon. He wanted the nation to see that he was someone people could trust. Gerald R. Ford had long been a member of Congress and was known as an honest, hardworking man. He often said these qualities were learned in his childhood.

Ford was president for less than two and a half years. But Ford had never expected to be president. "I look back and wonder how it ever happened to me," he once said.

29

President Ford announced his pardon of Richard Nixon on September 8, 1974, just one month after he entered office. The act angered many Americans, who felt that Nixon should have been punished for what he had done.

Ford is the only president who never won a national election.

One month after Ford became president, he made one of the most difficult decisions of his life. He wanted to help the country recover from the Watergate scandal. To do so, he decided to pardon Richard Nixon of all criminal charges. This meant that Nixon would not be tried or punished for the crimes of which he was accused.

Some people claimed that Ford had made a deal with the former president. After all, the two men had been friends for many years. But this was not the case. Ford simply believed that pardoning Nixon was the best way for the nation to move on and forget Watergate. He believed he was doing the best thing for the country by ending the matter quickly. Some people agreed, but many did not. "I have to say that most of my staff disagreed with me over the pardon," Ford said later. "But I was absolutely convinced that it was the right thing to do."

President Ford faced many other problems as well. He had little experience dealing with foreign affairs, the nation's dealings with other countries. **Inflation** was a serious problem as well. Prices were high on everything from food to housing. Many Americans were out of work. Gas and oil supplies were dwindling. Ford had entered office at a very difficult time. In addition, Congress was made up mostly of Democrats. They were against most of Ford's ideas because he was a Republican. He had to find ways to **compromise** on some issues. The ability to compromise allowed Ford to solve some problems in the United States. Inflation decreased, and more than four million unemployed Americans found jobs during his presidency.

Ford also worked to improve relations with other nations. He made goodwill trips to many foreign countries, including Japan, China, and a number of European nations. He hosted foreign leaders who came to observe the nation's bicentennial (its 200th birthday) in 1976. Henry Kissinger was Ford's secretary of state, which means that he was in charge of the nation's dealings with other countries. Kissinger worked to build and keep good relations with other nations.

Ford had to deal with another serious problem in May of 1975. In Asia, Cambodian gunboats seized an American merchant ship, the *Mayaguez*. Ford quickly

President Ford selected New York governor Nelson Rockefeller to be his vice president in 1974. He selected Robert Dole as his running mate in the 1976 presidential election.

Ford still considered Richard Nixon a friend after the Watergate scandal. "Nixon was a longtime friend who made a very stupid mistake," Ford once said. "Everyone is human and can make mistakes."

31

ordered U.S. forces to retake the ship. The *Mayaguez* and 39 crewmen were saved.

The next presidential election took place in 1976. Ford barely won the Republican nomination for president over Ronald Reagan of California. Ford and the vice presidential candidate, Robert Dole, ran against the Democratic candidate, Jimmy Carter. Ford lost to Carter in one of the closest presidential races in history. On January 20, 1977, President Carter graciously began his inauguration speech by praising President Ford: "For myself and for our nation, I want to thank my **predecessor** [President Ford] for all he has done to heal our land."

President and Mrs. Ford retired to their new home in Rancho Mirage, California. Ford wrote his memoirs in a book called *A Time to Heal: The Autobiography*

Two people tried to assassinate Ford while he was in office. Both of the would-be assassins were women.

Ford's daughter Susan held her senior prom at the White House.

In November of 1974, President Ford traveled to the Soviet Union to meet with Soviet premier Leonid Brezhnev (left). The two men discussed reducing their countries' **nuclear weapons.** *In 1976, the two countries signed an agreement to limit nuclear testing.*

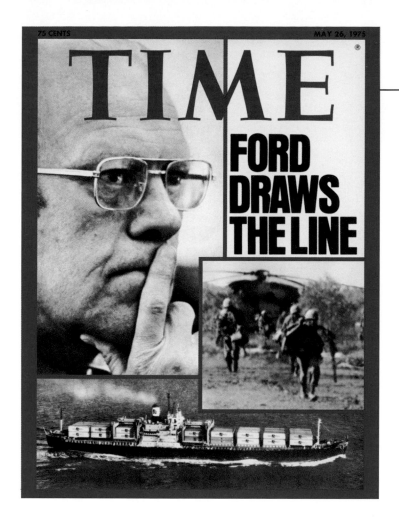

As this Time *magazine cover shows, one of the most serious crises of Ford's presidency was when **communist** forces in Cambodia seized an American ship called the* Mayaguez. *U.S. marines rescued the 39 members of the* Mayaguez *crew, but the cost was high. More than 40 soldiers were killed in the course of the rescue.*

of Gerald R. Ford. It was published in 1979. In 1981, the Gerald R. Ford Library in Ann Arbor and the Gerald R. Ford Museum in Grand Rapids opened to honor the former president. Ford toured the country giving speeches about politics and current issues. He also wrote another book, *Humor and the Presidency.*

Ford remained active in the Republican Party, traveling around the country to campaign for its candidates. He gave speeches at hundreds of colleges and universities about how the U.S. government works. In 1982, after many years of participating

Ford was the first U.S. president to visit Japan.

One night President Ford got up to walk his dog, Liberty, and accidentally locked himself out of the White House.

in the American Enterprise Institute (AEI), Ford organized and hosted the AEI World Forum. This gathering in Vail, Colorado, brought together a group of retired and current international world and business leaders. Their goal was to discuss and find better ways to solve political and business problems all around the world.

President Ford was the recipient of many awards. In August of 1999, President Bill Clinton presented him with the Presidential Medal of Freedom, the highest award the president can present to a U.S. citizen. It honored Gerald Ford for his role in the handling of the Watergate scandal and of Nixon's resignation. Two months later, in October of 1999, President and Mrs. Ford received the highest honor awarded by the U.S. Congress, the Congressional Gold Medal.

Gerald R. Ford died at his home in California on December 26, 2006. He was 93 years old, the oldest living former president to date. Funeral services were held in Rancho Mirage, California; Washington, D.C.; and Grand Rapids, Michigan; where he was laid to rest.

Gerald Ford was president for only about two and a half years, but during that time, he was able to restore Americans' faith in the nation's most important position. This may have been Ford's most significant accomplishment. When asked how he hoped his brief time in office would be remembered, the former president replied, "I hope historians will write that the Ford **administration** healed the land, that I restored public confidence in the White House and in government."

In 2000, 87-year-old Gerald Ford attended the National Convention of the Republican Party, where the party would select its presidential candidate. He was there to show his support for the presidential nominee, George W. Bush. While there, Ford suffered a stroke and was hospitalized. Within a week, he had recovered and was able to return home to California.

President Ford and his golden retriever, Liberty, in the Oval Office in 1974

BETTY FORD

As first lady, Betty Ford believed her role was to "see as many people as possible and tell them about the integrity, leadership, and honesty of the president." But she is also remembered for her support of the equal rights **amendment** (ERA). This proposed amendment to the **Constitution** promised equal rights to all women in the United States.

    Mrs. Ford believed women should have the same chances as men to get a good education, have a fulfilling career, or pursue other opportunities. She traveled around the country giving speeches and interviews about the ERA. She wrote letters to congresspeople urging them to pass it. Mrs. Ford also encouraged her husband to name women to important positions in the government. She believed that all women, whether devoted to motherhood or to a career outside the home, deserved equal rights and opportunities. Even her hard work didn't help make the ERA become law, however. It was not approved by enough states to become part of the Constitution.

Although Mrs. Ford was a hardworking first lady, she had many health problems. Years before, a pinched nerve ended her promising career as a dancer. Later, this problem became more serious, causing a great deal of pain. Then, in 1974, she underwent surgery for breast cancer. Mrs. Ford spoke publicly about her illness. She hoped this would help other women who battled the same disease. But through this difficult experience, Mrs. Ford was in terrible pain. To relieve it, she took medication and drank alcohol. Her use of these substances became an **addiction**.

In 1978, the Ford family confronted Betty about her addiction to alcohol and drugs. In April of that year, she agreed to seek treatment for her problem and entered a program at Long Beach Naval Hospital. This program—and her own determination—helped Mrs. Ford overcome addiction. After her recovery, she spoke openly about her problem. She hoped that her willingness to discuss it might encourage others with similar problems to get help. In 1987, a television movie was made about her life. That same year, she published a book, *Betty: A Glad Awakening*. Both told of Mrs. Ford's successful treatment.

In 1982, Mrs. Ford helped establish the Betty Ford Center in Rancho Mirage, California. This facility was founded to help people who suffer from alcohol and drug addiction. Today it is considered one of the best treatment centers in the world. It has helped nearly 40,000 people overcome addiction. Mrs. Ford continues to speak out about alcoholism and drug abuse. "As a recovering alcoholic woman," she says, "I know first hand how the disease of alcoholism and other drug addiction can affect the lives of families and loved ones. Sadly, there is still very little assistance available for anyone whose life has been touched by this disease." She hopes the Betty Ford Center will help to change this.

Time Line

| 1910–1920 | 1930 | 1940 | | 1950 |

1913
1913 Gerald R. Ford Jr. is born Leslie Lynch King Jr. on July 14.

1916
On February 1, Ford's mother, Dorothy, marries Gerald R. Ford Sr.

1927
At age 14, Ford achieves the rank of Eagle Scout and tries out for the high school football team.

1931
Ford enrolls at the University of Michigan at Ann Arbor.

1935
Ford graduates from the University of Michigan. On December 3, Leslie Lynch King Jr. legally changes his name to Gerald Rudolph Ford Jr.

1938
Yale University accepts Ford into its law school.

1941
Ford graduates from Yale University Law School in the top 25 percent of his class. On December 7, Japan bombs the U.S. naval base at Pearl Harbor in Hawaii. The United States enters World War II.

1942
Ford joins the U.S. Navy in April. His first assignment is as an athletic training officer, and his job is to keep the sailors in shape.

1943
Ford is assigned to an aircraft carrier, the USS *Monterey.* He is a gunnery officer and is also in charge of physical training for the ship's crew.

1944
In December, Ford nearly loses his life when the *Monterey* is caught in "The Great Typhoon."

1946
Ford is discharged from the navy.

1947
In August, Ford meets his future wife, Betty Bloomer Warren.

1948
On October 15, Gerald Ford and Betty Bloomer Warren are married. Ford is elected to the U.S. House of Representatives in November. He is reelected to the House for 12 more terms.

1951
Ford becomes a member of the House Appropriations Committee in the House of Representatives.

38

1961
Ford becomes a member of the Defense Appropriations Subcommittee in the House of Representatives.

1963
President John F. Kennedy is assassinated in November. Lyndon Johnson becomes president. Johnson names Ford to the Warren Commission, the group charged with investigating the assassination of President John F. Kennedy.

1965
Ford and John R. Stiles write a book, *Portrait of the Assassin*. Ford is elected the House minority leader.

1968
Ford supports Richard Nixon in the presidential election. Nixon is elected the 37th president of the United States.

1972
Nixon is reelected president.

1973
Nixon chooses Ford as his vice president after Spiro T. Agnew resigns.

1974
On August 9, President Richard Nixon resigns. Ford is sworn in as the 38th president of the United States. On August 20, President Ford selects former governor of New York Nelson A. Rockefeller to be the vice president. On September 8, President Ford pardons Nixon, which means that Nixon will not be tried or punished for his involvement in the Watergate scandal. This act angers many Americans. On November 17, President Ford departs for a visit to Japan. It is the first visit by a U.S. President to that country. He also visits South Korea and the Soviet Union.

1975
On May 12, Cambodia seizes a U.S. merchant ship, the *Mayaguez*. President Ford orders military action, and the ship and crew are rescued. On July 19, President Ford formally announces his candidacy for election in 1976.

1976
The Republican Party nominates Ford as their candidate. On November 2, President Ford loses the presidential election. Jimmy Carter is elected the 39th president.

1979
President Ford publishes his memoirs, *A Time to Heal: The Autobiography of Gerald R. Ford.*

1981
President Ford dedicates the Gerald R. Ford Presidential Library in Ann Arbor, Michigan and the Gerald R. Ford Presidential Museum in Grand Rapids, Michigan.

1982
The Betty Ford Center is dedicated.

1987
Ford writes another book, *Humor and the Presidency*.

1994
The University of Michigan retires President Ford's football jersey number (48).

1999
In August, President Clinton presents Gerald Ford with the Presidential Medal of Freedom. In October, President and Mrs. Ford receive the Congressional Gold Medal, the highest award given by Congress.

2000
In July, Ford suffers a stroke while attending the Republican Party National Convention. He is hospitalized but recovers in one week.

2001
The John F. Kennedy Foundation presents Ford with the Profiles in Courage Award.

2004
Ford attends the groundbreaking for the Ford School of Public Policy at the University of Michigan.

2006
The NCAA names President Ford as the 14th most influential student athlete of the last 100 years.

2006
On December 26, Gerald R. Ford dies at the age of 93. He was the longest-living former president to date.

G L O S S A R Y

addiction (uh-DIK-shun) An addiction is a habit that a person cannot give up. Betty Ford suffered an addiction to alcohol and drugs.

administration (ad-min-ih-STRAY-shun) An administration is the time during which a person holds office. Ford hoped his administration had restored confidence in the presidency.

aircraft carrier (AYR-kraft KAYR-ee-ur) An aircraft carrier is a ship with a large, flat deck from which aircraft take off and land. Ford served on an aircraft carrier during World War II.

amendment (uh-MEND-ment) An amendment is a change or addition made to the U.S. Constitution. The Equal Rights Amendment promised equal rights to American women.

assassinated (uh-SASS-ih-nay-ted) When a well-known person is murdered, he or she has been assassinated. After President Kennedy was assassinated, Ford became part of a committee that investigated the assassination.

campaign (kam-PAYN) A campaign is the process of running for an election, including activities such as giving speeches or attending rallies. Ford kept his campaign for the House of Representatives a secret for many months.

candidate (KAN-dih-det) A candidate is a person running in an election. The Republicans chose Ford as their candidate for Congress in 1948.

communist (KOM-yoo-nist) Communist describes a system of government in which the central government, not the people, holds all the power. Many Americans were afraid of communism after World War II. During Ford's presidency, communist forces in Cambodia seized an American ship.

compromise (KOM-pruh-myz) A compromise is a way to settle a disagreement in which both sides give up part of what they want. Ford was able to compromise with his opponents in Congress during his presidency.

constitution (kon-stih-TOO-shun) A constitution is the set of basic principles that govern a state, country, or society. The equal rights amendment did not become part of the U.S. Constitution.

convention (kuhn-VEN-shuhn) In politics, a convention is a large meeting where party candidates are chosen. Ford supported his friend Richard Nixon at the Republican National Convention in 1968.

discharged (DIS-charjd) To be discharged means to be released. Ford was discharged from the navy in 1946.

ensign (EN-sin) An ensign is a low-ranking officer in the navy. Ford accepted a position as an ensign when he began training in the navy.

hangar deck (HANG-uhr DEK) The hangar deck is the deck on an aircraft carrier where the aircraft are stored.

impeach (im-PEECH) If the House of Representatives votes to impeach, it charges the president with a crime or serious misdeed. Congress prepared to impeach President Nixon in 1974.

inauguration (ih-nawg-yuh-RAY-shun) An inauguration is the ceremony that takes place when a new president begins a term. Ford's inauguration took place on August 9, 1974.

inflation (in-FLAY-shun) Inflation is a sharp and sudden rise in the price of goods. Inflation was a serious problem when Gerald Ford became president.

isolationism (ice-uh-LAY-shun-iz-um) Isolationism is a country's policy of staying out of the affairs of other countries. The United States had a policy of isolationism before World War II.

minority (mye-NOR-uh-tee) Minority means a small number or part within a larger group. In 1965, when Republicans were the minority group in the House of Representatives, Ford became the House minority leader.

navigator (NAV-ih-gay-tur) A navigator is a person who determines the position and course of a ship, airplane, or other craft. Ford was an assistant navigator during World War II.

Nazi Party (NAHT-see PAR-tee) The Nazi Party was a political party that ruled Germany from 1933 to 1945. The Nazis blamed other countries and races for the problems that Germany faced after World War I.

nomination (nom-ih-NAY-shun) If someone receives a nomination, he or she is chosen by a political party to run for an office. To run for Congress, Ford had to win the Republican Party nomination.

nuclear weapons (NOO-klee-ur WEP-uhns) Nuclear weapons are weapons that used the power created by splitting atoms. Ford and Soviet leader Leonid Brezhnev signed an agreement to limit the testing of nuclear weapons.

officer (AW-feh-ser) An officer is a leader in the military who commands other soldiers. Ford's first assignment in the navy was as an athletic training officer.

political parties (puh-LIT-ih-kul PAR-teez) Political parties are groups of people who share similar ideas about how to run a government. The Republican Party is one of the nation's two most powerful political parties.

politician (pawl-ih-TISH-un) A politician is a person who holds an office in government. Ford was a politician.

politics (PAWL-uh-tiks) Politics refers to the actions and practices of the government. In 1948, Ford began his career in politics.

predecessor (PRED-eh-ses-ur) A predecessor is someone who holds a position or office before another person. Ford was President Carter's predecessor.

promoted (pruh-MOH-ted) People who are promoted receive a more important job or position to recognize their good work. While in the navy, Ford was quickly promoted from ensign to lieutenant.

Republican Party (re-PUB-lih-kun PAR-tee) The Republican Party is one of two major poltiical parties in the United States. Gerald Ford was a member of the Republican Party.

resigned (ree-ZINED) A person who resigned from a job gave it up. Ford became vice president after Spiro Agnew resigned from office.

scandal (SKAN-dul) A scandal is a shameful action that shocks the public. When President Nixon was involved in dishonest activities, it was considered a scandal.

term (TERM) A term is the length of time a politician can keep his or her position by law. A U.S. president's term is four years.

THE UNITED STATES GOVERNMENT

The United States government is divided into three equal branches: the executive, the legislative, and the judicial. This division helps prevent abuses of power because each branch has to answer to the other two. No one branch can become too powerful.

EXECUTIVE BRANCH

PRESIDENT
VICE PRESIDENT
DEPARTMENTS

The job of the executive branch is to enforce the laws. It is headed by the president, who serves as the spokesperson for the United States around the world. The president signs bills into law and appoints important officials such as federal judges. He or she is also the commander in chief of the U.S. military. The president is assisted by the vice president, who takes over if the president dies or cannot carry out the duties of the office.

The executive branch also includes various departments, each focused on a specific topic. They include the Defense Department, the Justice Department, and the Agriculture Department. The department heads, along with other officials such as the vice president, serve as the president's closest advisers, called the cabinet.

LEGISLATIVE BRANCH

CONGRESS
Senate and
House of Representatives

The job of the legislative branch is to make the laws. It consists of Congress, which is divided into two parts: the Senate and the House of Representatives. The Senate has 100 members, and the House of Representatives has 435 members. Each state has two senators. The number of representatives a state has varies depending on the state's population.

Besides making laws, Congress also passes budgets and enacts taxes. In addition, it is responsible for declaring war, maintaining the military, and regulating trade with other countries.

JUDICIAL BRANCH

SUPREME COURT
COURTS OF APPEALS
DISTRICT COURTS

The job of the judicial branch is to interpret the laws. It consists of the nation's federal courts. Trials are held in district courts. During trials, judges must decide what laws mean and how they apply. Courts of appeals review the decisions made in district courts.

The nation's highest court is the Supreme Court. If someone disagrees with a court of appeals ruling, he or she can ask the Supreme Court to review it. The Supreme Court may refuse. The Supreme Court makes sure that decisions and laws do not violate the Constitution.

CHOOSING
THE PRESIDENT

It may seem odd, but American voters don't elect the president directly. Instead, the president is chosen using what is called the Electoral College.

Each state gets as many votes in the Electoral College as its combined total of senators and representatives in Congress. For example, Iowa has two senators and five representatives, so it gets seven electoral votes. Although the District of Columbia does not have any voting members in Congress, it gets three electoral votes. Usually, the candidate who wins the most votes in any given state receives all of that state's electoral votes.

To become president, a candidate must get more than half of the Electoral College votes. There are a total of 538 votes in the Electoral College, so a candidate needs 270 votes to win. If nobody receives 270 Electoral College votes, the House of Representatives chooses the president.

With the Electoral College system, the person who receives the most votes nationwide does not always receive the most electoral votes. This happened most recently in 2000, when Al Gore received half a million more national votes than George W. Bush. Bush became president because he had more Electoral College votes.

THE WHITE HOUSE

The White House is the official home of the president of the United States. It is located at 1600 Pennsylvania Avenue NW in Washington, D.C. In 1792, a contest was held to select the architect who would design the president's home. James Hoban won. Construction took eight years.

The first president, George Washington, never lived in the White House. The second president, John Adams, moved into the house in 1800, though the inside was not yet complete. During the War of 1812, British soldiers burned down much of the White House. It was rebuilt several years later.

The White House was changed through the years. Porches were added, and President Theodore Roosevelt added the West Wing. President William Taft changed the shape of the presidential office, making it into the famous Oval Office. While Harry Truman was president, the old house was discovered to be structurally weak. All the walls were reinforced with steel, and the rooms were rebuilt.

Today, the White House has 132 rooms (including 35 bathrooms), 28 fireplaces, and 3 elevators. It takes 570 gallons of paint to cover the outside of the six-story building. The White House provides the president with many ways to relax. It includes a putting green, a jogging track, a swimming pool, a tennis court, and beautifully landscaped gardens. The White House also has a movie theater, a billiard room, and a one-lane bowling alley.

PRESIDENTIAL PERKS

The job of president of the United States is challenging. It is probably one of the most stressful jobs in the world. Because of this, presidents are paid well, though not nearly as well as the leaders of large corporations. In 2007, the president earned $400,000 a year. Presidents also receive extra benefits that make the demanding job a little more appealing.

★ **Camp David:** In the 1940s, President Franklin D. Roosevelt chose this heavily wooded spot in the mountains of Maryland to be the presidential retreat, where presidents can relax. Even though it is a retreat, world business is conducted there. Most famously, President Jimmy Carter met with Middle Eastern leaders at Camp David in 1978. The result was a peace agreement between Israel and Egypt.

★ *Air Force One:* The president flies on a jet called *Air Force One*. It is a Boeing 747-200B that has been modified to meet the president's needs.

Air Force One is the size of a large home. It is equipped with a dining room, sleeping quarters, a conference room, and office space. It also has two kitchens that can provide food for up to 50 people.

★ **The Secret Service:** While not the most glamorous of the president's perks, the Secret Service is one of the most important. The Secret Service is a group of highly trained agents who protect the president and the president's family.

★ **The Presidential State Car:** The presidential limousine is a stretch Cadillac DTS.

It has been armored to protect the president in case of attack. Inside the plush car are a foldaway desk, an entertainment center, and a communications console.

★ **The Food:** The White House has five chefs who will make any food the president wants. The White House also has an extensive wine collection.

★ **Retirement:** A former president receives a pension, or retirement pay, of just under $180,000 a year. Former presidents also receive Secret Service protection for the rest of their lives.

F A C T S

QUALIFICATIONS

To run for president, a candidate must

* ★ be at least 35 years old
* ★ be a citizen who was born in the United States
* ★ have lived in the United States for 14 years

TERM OF OFFICE

A president's term of office is four years.
No president can stay in office for more than two terms.

ELECTION DATE

The presidential election takes place every four years on the first Tuesday of November.

INAUGURATION DATE

Presidents are inaugurated on January 20.

OATH OF OFFICE

I do solemnly swear I will faithfully execute the office of the President of the United States and will to the best of my ability preserve, protect, and defend the Constitution of the United States.

WRITE A LETTER TO THE PRESIDENT

One of the best things about being a U.S. citizen is that Americans get to participate in their government. They can speak out if they feel government leaders aren't doing their jobs. They can also praise leaders who are going the extra mile. Do you have something you'd like the president to do? Should the president worry more about the environment and encourage people to recycle? Should the government spend more money on our schools? You can write a letter to the president to say how you feel!

1600 Pennsylvania Avenue
Washington, D.C. 20500
You can even send an e-mail to: president@whitehouse.gov

BOOKS

Cohen, Daniel. *Watergate.* Brookfield, CT: Millbrook Press, 1998.

Ford, Betty. *The Times of My Life.* New York: Harper and Row, 1978.

Gaines, Ann Graham. *Richard M. Nixon.* Mankato, MN: The Child's World, 2009.

Santella, Andrew. *Gerald R. Ford.* Minneapolis: Compass Point Books, 2004.

Stein, R. Conrad. *Gerald R. Ford: America's 38th President.* New York: Children's Press, 2005.

Winget, Mary Mueller. *Gerald R. Ford.* Minneapolis, Twenty-First Century Books, 2007.

VIDEOS

The American President. DVD, VHS (Alexandria, VA: PBS Home Video, 2000).

Gerald R. Ford: Healing the Presidency (Biography). DVD (New York: A & E Home Video, 2006).

The History Channel Presents The Presidents. DVD (New York: A & E Home Video, 2005).

National Geographic's Inside the White House. DVD (Washington, D.C.: National Geographic Video, 2003).

INTERNET SITES

Visit our Web page for lots of links about Gerald R. Ford and other U.S. presidents:

http://www.childsworld.com/links

Note to Parents, Teachers, and Librarians: We routinely verify our Web links to make sure they are safe, active sites—so encourage your readers to check them out!

INDEX